Charles Darwin and Alfred Russel Wallace

Written by Anna Claybourne
Illustrated by Laszlo Veres

Contents

Collins

D0255707

Age of discovery

The 1800s were a great age of discovery, invention and ideas.
This was the century when telephones and flushing toilets,
photography and light bulbs were invented. Germs, **genes**, atoms
and radio waves were discovered – and much, much more.

One of the most important ideas from that time is called
"natural selection". It explains how living things evolve, or change
over time, and why there are so many different **species**. It was one
of the biggest breakthroughs in the history of science.

Charles Darwin in 1849

Amazingly, not one, but two great scientists both had this idea. They were both thinking about it at the same time, around the middle of the 1800s. They both worked on it for many years, each without knowing how closely their thoughts matched. The two scientists' names were Charles Darwin and Alfred Russel Wallace.

Today, it is Charles Darwin whose name is better known. However, they were both equally important in their day.

Alfred Russel Wallace in 1869

Darwin's early life

Charles Darwin was the older of the two men. He was born on
12 February 1809 in Shrewsbury, England. His father, Robert Darwin,
was a well-known doctor and his mother Susannah was from
the famous Wedgwood pottery-making family. His grandfather,
Erasmus Darwin, was also a doctor, as well as a poet and inventor.

As a small boy, Charles loved nature.
He liked collecting pebbles and
plants, and his mother taught
him how to identify different
flowers. But when he was
only eight, his mother died.
Aged nine, he went to a nearby
boarding school, along with his
13-year-old brother.

Darwin didn't do very well
at school. He didn't listen
to his teachers and he
hated Maths. His father told
him, "You will be a disgrace
to yourself and all
your family!"

Darwin's father wanted him to be a doctor. So in 1825, aged 16, he was sent to study medicine in Edinburgh, Scotland. He hated it! Charles wrote to one of his sisters that the lectures were dull, and he couldn't bear the sight of blood.

After two years, Charles's father let him give up medicine and sent him to Cambridge to train as a vicar instead. It was an equally hopeless plan. Charles couldn't be bothered to try hard at subjects that bored him. He later wrote that he was wasting his time there.

However, he did have a passionate interest – his love of nature. Soon, it would lead him around the world, and make him famous.

Wallace's childhood

Alfred Russel Wallace was born 14 years after Darwin, on 8 January 1823. His parents, Thomas Vere Wallace and Mary Ann Greenell, lived in Usk, a small town in Wales. Alfred was one of nine children.

When Alfred was five, the Wallaces moved to Hertford in England, where Alfred's father worked as a librarian. They never had quite enough money and life was a struggle. But Alfred had a happy childhood and loved reading and gardening.

Alfred went to Hertford Grammar School, a small school with only one room, until he was 14. Then he had to earn a living to help support his family.

Wallace's first job was working for his older brother William, who had a **surveying** business. Alfred learnt to measure areas of land and the heights of hills to make maps. He also learnt about the different rocks that make up the land, and found lots of fossils. Alfred loved working outside, surrounded by nature.

After working for William, Alfred's skills helped him find other jobs, including teaching in a school and working on plans for a railway. However, just like Darwin, his true interests lay elsewhere.

A love of nature

As their lives went on, Darwin and Wallace both became more and more fascinated with the natural world. They filled their spare time with watching wildlife and reading about nature.

Charles Darwin may have been a lazy student, but he was devoted to his hobbies. He loved riding and walking in the countryside, spotting plants and animals. In Edinburgh, he often went to the seashore to collect interesting creatures from rock pools. In Cambridge, he started a new hobby – collecting beetles – and became almost obsessed with it.

Once, he found three beetles together. Desperate to catch them all, he held one in each hand and put the third in his mouth – a big mistake! "To my unspeakable disgust and pain," he wrote to a friend, "the little **inconsiderate** beast squirted his acid down my throat!" He had to spit it out, and dropped the other two in shock.

At university, Darwin made friends who helped him with his interests. One was Robert Grant, who became a leading **biologist**. Another, John Edmonstone, taught Darwin taxidermy – the art of stuffing and preserving dead animals.

Nature collectors

Today, people know not to collect things like wild animals and birds' eggs, as it harms them. In the 1800s, people saw things differently. **Naturalists** often caught and killed insects, for example, and preserved them in order to study them. In those days, plants and animals were less likely to be endangered and there were no laws against collecting wildlife specimens.

A head for science

Alfred Russel Wallace had always loved all kinds of learning.
Whenever he had any spare time, he read as much as he could.
He devoured the latest books on geology – how rocks shape
the Earth – and biology – the science of living things.

He was fascinated with "transmutation", which is now called
evolution. This is the idea that species of living things change over
time. Several scientists had spoken about it, but no one knew how
it happened and many people disagreed about it.

Wallace also read works by
Thomas Malthus on what makes
human populations rise and fall,
and by Charles Lyell on how rocks
form and wear away. In fact,
these were to be very important
in both Wallace's and Darwin's
future discoveries. They just
didn't know it at
the time.

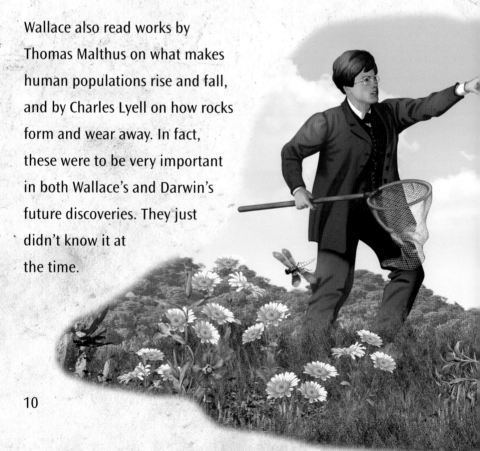

In 1844, while working as a teacher, Wallace spent his evenings at the local library. There, by chance, he met another nature fan, Henry Walter Bates. Bates was only 19, two years younger than Wallace, but he was already an experienced insect collector. He had even had an article published in a nature magazine.

When Bates showed him his beetle and butterfly collections, Wallace immediately wanted to start collecting too. He bought himself a set of insect-catching gear and the two men began going collecting together. Their friendship was to change the course of Wallace's life forever.

Adventurers

In the 1800s, there were many parts of the world – and many forms of wildlife – still waiting to be discovered. Naturalists and explorers roamed the globe, searching for exciting new species. They sold their specimens to museums such as London's Natural History Museum, to be stored and studied. Wallace and Darwin, both crazy about collecting wildlife, dreamt of what they might find in foreign lands.

Both men were inspired by the writings of a famous explorer, Alexander von Humboldt. He had explored South America and other lands with his companion Aimé Bonpland, between 1799 and 1804. They made all kinds of natural discoveries and wrote about their adventures. Their tales of tropical plants, huge insects, towering mountains and rushing jungle rivers excited both the would-be explorers.

Alexander von Humboldt

To the tropics!

In his last year at Cambridge, Darwin became close friends with
a **botany** professor, John Stevens Henslow. Henslow helped Darwin
with his nature studies and encouraged him to read Humboldt's
works. In 1831, longing to see tropical wildlife for himself, Darwin
hatched a plan to travel to the island of Tenerife.

Wallace also wanted to travel, after reading the works of Humboldt
and other explorers. Around 1847, he and Bates decided to go on
an expedition to South America themselves. They would collect
specimens and sell them to museums, as a way of making money
to pay for their trip.

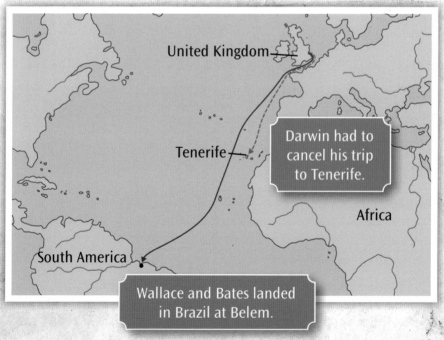

United Kingdom

Tenerife

Darwin had to
cancel his trip
to Tenerife.

Africa

South America

Wallace and Bates landed
in Brazil at Belem.

In December 1831, Charles Darwin did finally go on an adventure, just as he had planned. But it was far bigger and wilder than he had ever imagined.

In August 1831, Darwin returned to his father's house after a trip to Wales. Waiting for him was a letter from his friend Professor Henslow. In it, Henslow said he had been asked to recommend a naturalist to sail on a survey ship to South America. The job involved studying geology and collecting wildlife specimens, and being a companion for the ship's captain, Robert FitzRoy. Henslow thought Darwin was "the very man" and had suggested him!

HMS Beagle

It was a golden opportunity for Darwin to follow his dreams. But his father, who would have to pay his expenses, was not impressed, and refused. Luckily, Darwin's uncle persuaded him to change his mind. At last he agreed to let his son go on the trip.

Darwin went to meet FitzRoy and they got on well. Soon, everything was arranged. Just after Christmas 1831, Darwin set sail on the *HMS Beagle*. It was to be his home for the next five years.

Darwin's nose

Darwin later learnt that FitzRoy almost rejected him because of his nose! In those days, there was a belief that the shapes of people's faces showed their personalities. FitzRoy thought Darwin's round nose meant he was weak and lazy. Luckily, FitzRoy decided to ignore his worries.

15

The voyage of the *Beagle* was the most exciting thing that could possibly have happened to the 22-year-old Charles Darwin. He worked harder than ever before, collecting specimens and making endless notes and sketches.

The *Beagle's* mission was to chart the coast of South America, making maps for the British government. Her voyage took her across the Atlantic Ocean to Brazil, then around South America. She visited Uruguay, Argentina, Chile and the Galapagos Islands. From there, she sailed on across the Pacific Ocean, returning home via Australia and Africa – a five-year, round-the-world trip.

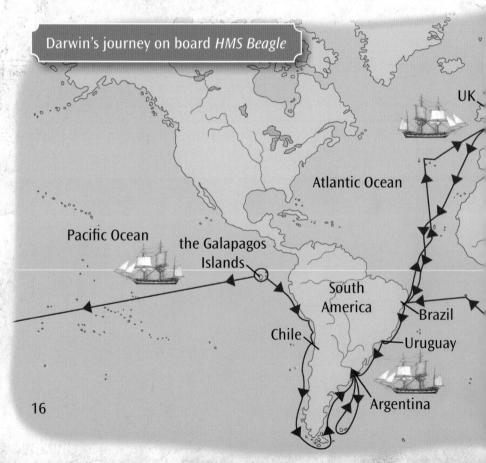

Darwin's journey on board *HMS Beagle*

This epic journey gave Darwin the chance to encounter all kinds of incredible plants and animals, rocks and fossils.

Throughout his voyage, Darwin wrote to friends and family. One of his first letters was to his father, written after stopping at the Cape Verde islands. He exclaimed, "My eyes have already feasted on the exquisite form and colours of cocoa nuts, bananas and the beautiful orange trees … "

Henslow collected his letters from Darwin and made them into a booklet, which he showed to other nature experts.

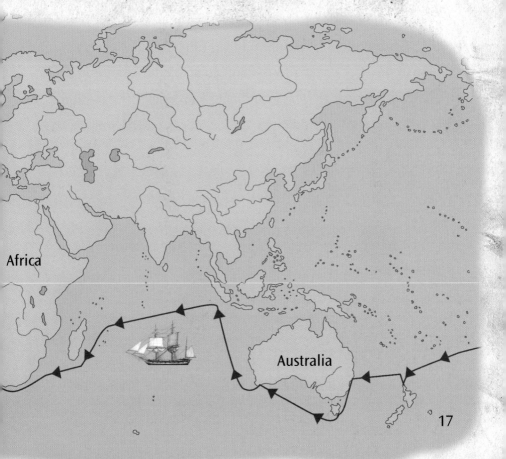

Africa

Australia

Darwin comes home

In 1836, the *Beagle* finally completed her journey and returned to England. Charles Darwin was now 27 and had learnt a huge amount from his experiences. However, he still liked playing tricks on his older sisters.

Charles arrived back at his family home late at night. Instead of waking everyone up, he sneaked off to bed. Then, in the morning, he walked in and surprised everyone while they were having breakfast!

Soon, Darwin began to wonder if it was time for him to get married. Famously, he wrote a list of **pros and cons** to help him decide. One of the pros was that he would have "a constant companion – better than a dog, anyhow"!

Darwin didn't want to turn into a boring old man who did nothing but work.
He proposed to his cousin, Emma Wedgwood, in November 1838 and they married in 1839. They soon moved to the village of Downe in Kent.

Emma Wedgwood

Darwin and his wife went on to have ten children. In those days, men didn't always spend much time with their children. Darwin, though, turned out to be a very loving, caring father. He played and joked with his children, and loved chatting to them and teaching them about nature.

Following in Darwin's footsteps

The *Beagle's* voyage lasted from 1831 to 1836, when Darwin was in his twenties. As he was 14 years older than Wallace, his great journey was over before Wallace's began.

In fact, before Wallace went exploring with Bates, he had heard of Darwin and read about his *Beagle* adventures. The two men did not know each other yet, but their paths were growing closer.

On 26 April 1848, Bates and Wallace sailed for Brazil in South America. They planned to collect wildlife specimens, but Wallace also had another aim. He was still interested in transmutation – or evolution – and hoped to find evidence for how species changed over time.

Just like Darwin, Wallace was thrilled by the variety of life in the tropics. He and Bates set to work, collecting and studying beetles and butterflies, birds, flowers and trees.

However, the two men had different interests and soon agreed to explore separately. Wallace spent the next three years in the Amazon jungle, collecting thousands of specimens. He also mapped parts of the Amazon River, using the surveying skills he learnt with his brother.

In 1852, Wallace decided to take his collections back to the UK. But disaster struck. The ship he sailed on, the *Helen*, caught fire and sank! Wallace and the crew were rescued after ten days in a lifeboat. But his precious specimens, notes and sketches were lost at the bottom of the sea.

Wallace made it home safely. Luckily his possessions were insured and he received some money to live on. His horrible experience at sea hadn't put him off exploring. On the contrary, he began planning another trip. Meanwhile, he wrote articles and books about the Amazon and became a well-known naturalist.

It was in 1853, before Wallace set off on his second voyage, that Wallace and Darwin met for the first time. At this time, Darwin was 44 and had settled down with his wife and family. Wallace was 30 and still a young adventurer. However, they were both respected scientists and knew many of the same people. Wallace later wrote that he had bumped into Darwin for just a few minutes, at the British Museum in London. A few years later, in 1856, they started writing to each other.

In 1854, Wallace set off on his travels once more. This time, he went to the Malay Archipelago, in Southeast Asia – a group of islands that includes modern Indonesia and parts of Malaysia. The jungles there were known for their exotic birds, insects and other wildlife.

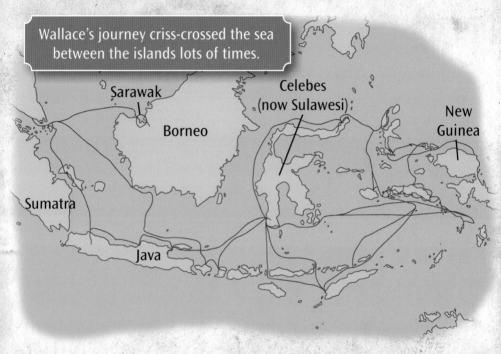

Wallace's journey criss-crossed the sea between the islands lots of times.

Sarawak
Celebes (now Sulawesi)
New Guinea
Borneo
Sumatra
Java

This journey lasted eight years, until 1862, and was a huge achievement for Wallace. He explored the whole region, making more than 20,000 kilometres of jungle and island journeys. He collected over 100,000 insects, 7,000 seashells and 8,000 birds.

At the same time, Wallace was thinking hard about the puzzle of evolution. It was here, on a remote island in Indonesia, that a huge and important idea would occur to him.

Wallace at home

When Wallace returned from Asia in 1862, he was almost 40. In 1864, he met Annie Mitten. The daughter of his friend William Mitten, Annie was 23 years younger than Wallace. They married in 1866, when she was 20 and he was 43.

Annie Mitten

Alfred and Annie Wallace had three children. Like Darwin, Wallace loved being a father. He spent lots of time with his children and often wrote to them when he was away. Later, they recalled that his work as a naturalist was great fun for them when they were little. They said that Wallace had kept a live lizard in his study and they were allowed to run in and out while he worked.

Sadly, Wallace's oldest son died of scarlet fever when he was six. This disease can be treated today, but long ago it often killed people.

Wallace with one of his children

Apart from this sadness, though, Alfred and Annie Wallace had a long and happy marriage. Like her husband, Annie loved nature, and the couple often spent hours gardening together. Sometimes, Annie also helped him with organising and writing up his books and papers.

Wild discoveries!

Charles Darwin spent five years on the voyage of the *Beagle*. Alfred Russel Wallace explored for even longer – his two trips added up to 12 years abroad. During their travels, both men discovered plants and animals previously unknown to science.

When scientists back in England studied the specimens Darwin had discovered, they often named the new species after him.

This forest frog, discovered by Darwin in Chile, has a strange pointy nose. It was named 'Darwin's frog'.

Darwin had heard of a rare bird called a rhea from locals in Argentina. He searched for a specimen of it, but had no luck. Then, as the *Beagle's* crew were having a meal, Darwin realised they were eating one of the rare birds he was looking for! Another crew member had shot it for dinner. Darwin saved the bones to be send to London. The species is now known as "Darwin's rhea".

Wallace also discovered his very own frog, along with thousands of other living things that were new to science.

Wallace collected this beautiful beetle in New Guinea.

Wallace's jewel beetle

Wallace's flying frog

This rare bird is one of Southeast Asia's many beautiful birds of paradise. Wallace found it in Indonesia, and it was one of the discoveries he was most proud of.

Wallace's standardwing

When Wallace and Bates visited South America in 1848, they noticed something interesting. Insects like beetles and caterpillars often had very bright, vivid colours and patterns. Having bright colours seems strange for something like a caterpillar, as it makes it easier for birds and lizards to see and catch it.

However, Bates and Wallace found that the most colourful creatures also smelt bad, or released painful chemicals. Much later, when discussing this with Darwin, Wallace saw that it did make sense. The bright colours were a way of warning hunters not to even try eating the nasty-tasting bugs.

Wallace's discovery is now known as "warning colouration". It can be seen in many other animals too, like octopuses, wasps and tiny poison frogs.

This caterpillar has bright colours to warn away predators.

Separately, Darwin and Wallace both discovered another very interesting fact about living things. Wherever they went on their travels, they found species of animals arranged in groups and patterns. The patterns seemed to have a lot to do with geography – the layout of the land, mountains, rivers and islands.

Darwin found one example of this when he visited the Galapagos Islands in the Pacific Ocean. Darwin learnt that different islands in the group had their own different types of giant tortoise. Some were bigger, some smaller. Some had longer necks, and the different types had different shell shapes too. From his studies and talking to the locals, Darwin saw that this also applied to other creatures, such as finches and mockingbirds.

Pinta Island

Isabela Island

Hood Island

In 1853, Wallace wrote an article about the monkeys he had seen in the Amazon rainforest. He had noticed that different species of monkeys lived on opposite sides of large rivers, such as the Rio Negro.

black-headed uakari

black spider monkey

North

Rio Negro

South

Humboldt's woolly monkey

red-whiskered pithecia

In Southeast Asia, Wallace again found something similar. Species were different on either side of an invisible line across the Malay Archipelago, now known as the "Wallace line".

Fossil finds

Fossils were big news in the 1800s. Scientists had only recently started to study them, and often argued about what they meant. Did they show animals changing from one form to another over time?

When Darwin found interesting fossils on his travels, he thought about this. He saw that fossil animals weren't totally different from living ones. They were more like different versions of them.

For example, when Darwin found the fossil jawbone of a giant sloth, it wasn't a mysterious, alien creature – it was a sloth. It was different to today's sloths – it was bigger, stronger, and lived on the ground instead of in the trees. But they came from the same areas and seemed to be related.

two-toed sloth found in South America today

Darwin's ground sloth

Darwin also thought about rheas, the flightless birds of South America. One species, the greater rhea, was common further north. As the *Beagle* headed south, the smaller "Darwin's rhea" became more common. They changed over distance, as the sloths seemed to change through time.

South America

greater rhea

the smaller Darwin's rhea

There was so much to take in, it was hard to make sense of at first. Collecting, listing and sketching specimens was the most important job. But while Wallace was in the jungle and Darwin was back at home with his notes and journals, both men thought about their findings. They kept wondering what they could mean. Slowly, they were collecting evidence for the idea that would make them famous.

Big questions

For both Charles Darwin and Alfred Russel Wallace, there was one big, burning issue – the origin of species, or how species start.

There are millions of different species of living things. Wallace and Darwin spent years learning about these species. They studied thousands of bugs, birds, frogs, fish, trees, flowers and other living things of all kinds. They were among the leading experts on species in the world.

What both men really wanted to know was: where did species come from? How could there be so many, and how did a species start? And if new species did come from somewhere, what came before? Did one species actually change into another?

This might simply sound like an interesting puzzle for scientists to solve. In fact, it was much more than that. These questions didn't just affect science – they also affected religion.

There are thousands of species of butterflies.

Several scientists thought there was evidence that living things did change – especially from looking at fossils. Evolution, or change over time, seemed to make scientific sense.

However, according to Christianity and some other religions, this could not be possible. These religions stated that God had made all the world's living things and put them on the Earth just as they are now. Of course, that included human beings too.

The idea that living things could evolve was not new – it had been around since ancient Greek times. In modern Europe, though, most people believed in God's creation. Scientists tried to arrange plants and animals into fixed types, which were seen as God's deliberate design.

However, in the 1700s, other ideas returned, especially as the study of fossils took off.

In the 1740s, the French mathematician and **philosopher** Pierre Maupertuis wrote that creatures could change gradually, according to how good they were at surviving.

ammonite fossil

French naturalist George-Louis Leclerc thought that lots of species could develop from a smaller number of species.

Darwin's own grandfather, Erasmus Darwin, said that all animals could have come from one single creature, long ago.

The theory of evolution?

Around 1800, a scientist named Jean-Baptiste Lamarck came up with a complete theory of evolution. He said that living things, such as giraffes, changed to suit their surroundings better, then passed on their features to their babies. Lamarck wasn't quite right about how evolution happened, but his ideas were very important. They paved the way for a more scientific approach to the puzzle of evolution.

Lamarck thought that early giraffes had to stretch a lot to reach the food they liked best.

He reasoned that this stretched their necks, which got longer.

He believed that they passed on the new, long necks to their young.

The changing Earth

At the same time, other scientists were studying the Earth's rocks and landforms. They saw that the Earth itself seemed to have changed – not just its living things. James Hutton, a naturalist and geologist, had described this in the 1700s and the geologist Charles Lyell in the 1800s. They showed that:

- Seashell fossils were found high up on mountains, meaning that the seabed had moved.
- Glaciers and rivers could carry rocks long distances.
- Wind and rain wore mountains away.
- Layers of sand and sediment formed new rocks under the sea.
- Volcanoes moved rock out from inside the Earth.

a glacier

Some people, especially **clergymen**, objected to these ideas of change. Suggesting that the world and its living things could evolve challenged the Bible and other holy texts.

Some scientists agreed with this too. For example, Georges Cuvier was a top fossil expert in the early 1800s. His work proved that some animals had become extinct in the past. Yet Cuvier didn't believe in evolution. He claimed that animals died out because of disasters, such as floods, and God made new ones to replace them.

Some Christians had tried to work out exactly how long it had been since God created the world, according to the Bible. They thought the Earth was only around 6,000 years old. Scientists such as Hutton and Lyell said that as the Earth's rocks changed so slowly, it must be much, much older than that – millions of years old. They couldn't both be right!

Not all Christians thought this way, though. Many agreed that it was possible to be religious *and* scientific – and that all the Bible might not be literally true.

The Earth and the Sun

The church had been wrong before. The Bible says the Earth doesn't move – but in the 1500s and 1600s it had been proved that the Earth orbits the Sun. By Darwin and Wallace's time, most people accepted this – even Christians.

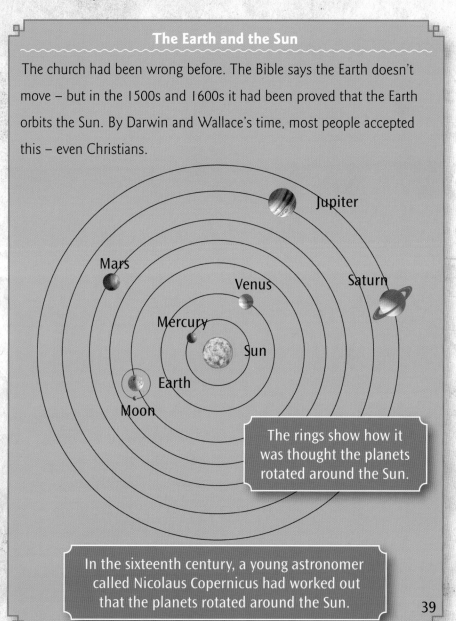

Jupiter

Mars

Venus

Saturn

Mercury

Sun

Earth

Moon

The rings show how it was thought the planets rotated around the Sun.

In the sixteenth century, a young astronomer called Nicolaus Copernicus had worked out that the planets rotated around the Sun.

After Darwin returned from the voyage of the *Beagle* in 1836, he settled down to sort out his ideas and write about his adventures. He worked through his notes and discoveries and asked himself what they meant. They led him to one sure conclusion. In March 1837, he scribbled it in his notebook: "One species does change into another."

That July, he also drew a famous diagram, now known as "Darwin's tree of life". At the top he wrote "I think" – then sketched a tree-like pattern. It showed how different groups and species might be like the branches and twigs of a tree, all related – some closely, some further apart.

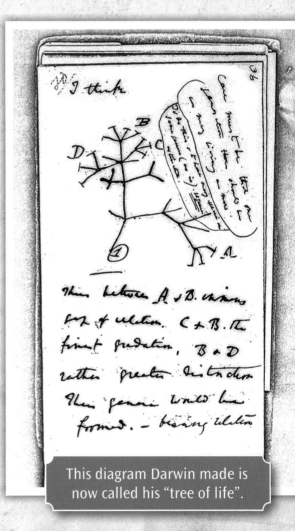

The tree also showed how today's species had "branched off" from earlier ones. Darwin's big idea was starting to form. He was to work on it for many years.

This diagram Darwin made is now called his "tree of life".

Like Darwin, Wallace had lots of facts and lots of questions, but it took a while for him to put them all together. For much of the 1850s, he was hard at work in the faraway jungles of Asia. He had little spare time, but he continued to think about species.

Wallace decided, as Darwin had, that different species of living things must be related to each other and that they changed gradually through time and over distance.

Unbeknown to each other, Darwin and Wallace were now working on almost exactly the same ideas.

Darwin's answer

Darwin later said that it was reading the work of Thomas Malthus in 1838 that helped his ideas to fall into place.

Malthus had written a book in 1798. In it, he wrote how people tended to have too many children. If there were too many people, he said, there would not be enough food for everyone, so humans would have to struggle against each other to survive.

Darwin saw that animals and plants did the same thing. They made too many young, eggs or seeds – far more than they needed to replace themselves.

This meant that only some could survive. Those that were best suited to surviving were "selected" by nature. And this meant that a species could change, as nature "selected" only the individuals with the most useful features. Darwin was to call this idea "natural selection".

Darwin felt his idea was so important and far-reaching, it should be written up as a big, detailed book. But to write and publish such a book, he needed more evidence. He spent 20 years working on his theory and planning his great work. In that time, Alfred Russel Wallace caught up with him.

Wallace's answer

Far away in Asia, Alfred Russel Wallace spent the 1850s chasing wildlife and thinking about species. By now, like Darwin, he was sure that life, and new species, did evolve.

In 1855 in Sarawak, Borneo, Wallace wrote an article spelling out his ideas on species so far. He sent it to Britain, where it was published in a **natural history** magazine.

The paper did not explain how evolution happened – Wallace had not got that far yet. But it did say that every time a new species appeared, it was closely related to another species living nearby, or to a species that had existed just before it. This statement has become known as the "Sarawak law". It was an important step that helped Wallace work his way towards how evolution happened.

Darwin's friend, the geologist Charles Lyell, saw Wallace's article. Lyell himself didn't think evolution was true. But the essay impressed him and he told Darwin about it. He saw that Wallace and Darwin were thinking along the same lines. If Darwin didn't hurry up with his book, Lyell said, Wallace might beat him to it!

Darwin didn't think Wallace's ideas were quite the same as his own, but in 1856, the two began writing to each other. Darwin told Wallace he had been preparing a book about the origin of species (how species start) for many years.

Wallace asked if Darwin would include the human species in his book. This was a daring idea, as the belief that God had created humans was central to Christianity. Darwin said he would avoid that topic for the time being.

In February 1858, on a remote island in Indonesia, Wallace came down with a fever.

Lying in bed, he could do little but think. Like Darwin, he began to think about the works of Thomas Malthus, which he had read as a young man.

Jungle fever

Wallace's fever was probably caused by malaria, a disease spread by mosquito bites. It is common in hot, damp places and can sometimes be deadly. Malaria is still a big problem in tropical areas today.

Did Malthus's work on humans relate to his own ideas on species?

All at once, Wallace realised how evolution worked. Just like Darwin, he saw that each generation of living things had too many individuals to survive. Only some – the best at surviving – would live to pass on their qualities to their young. And in this way, a species would become better at surviving and would change over time.

Sharing ideas

As soon as he was well enough, Wallace wrote down his ideas. He got
the whole theory on to paper as quickly and clearly as he could.
But what should he do next?

Wallace realised there was one man who could help him –
Charles Darwin. He was in England and shared Wallace's interests.
He was friends with the great scientist Charles Lyell, and might show
him the paper too. Wallace decided to send Darwin his new essay.

Natural selection

What exactly is natural selection and how does it work?

To understand Wallace and Darwin's big idea, you need to start with how species reproduce, or have young.

All living things have to reproduce. This means they have young that are copies of themselves, so that their species can carry on when they die. For example, an oak tree's acorns grow into new oak trees, dolphins give birth to baby dolphins, and lizards lay eggs that hatch into baby lizards.

Most living things make lots of seeds, eggs or young – more than enough to replace themselves. Usually, they do not all make it to adulthood. For example, a lizard might have 20 babies, but not all will survive. Quite a few will be caught and eaten by birds, snakes or other hunters before they grow up.

What decides which ones get eaten? It's partly just luck. But as in any family, there are also likely to be slight differences between the baby lizards. They may have different colours and patterns. Some may run faster than others. Some may be better at surviving cold weather.

The most useful features are the ones which make the lizards most likely to survive. For example, if the lizards are living in a green mountain meadow, lizards with greenish skin have a better chance. They have the best camouflage so hunters are less likely to spot them.

Next, the surviving lizards grow up and have their own young. Living things pass on their features to their young. So, if mostly green lizards survive, more green ones will be born.

This happens again and again. Gradually, the species becomes mostly green. You end up with a species of lizard that is perfectly camouflaged in its meadow home. This explains how species can change over time.

Evolution means changing in this way, gradually, step-by-step and by chance. The lizards did not change on purpose. It happened by accident. The meadow has green lizards in it simply because they were the ones that did best in that **habitat**.

This explains why, wherever you go, you find species that are perfectly suited, or adapted, to surviving in their habitat.

This moth is so perfectly camouflaged, it is hard to see in its habitat.

The origin of species

Darwin and Wallace were also interested in how new species came about. Natural selection answers this too.

If the lizard family lived at the edge of the meadow, next to some rocky mountain slopes, there would be two different habitats: the meadow and the rocky slope. The lizards that stayed in the meadow might evolve to become mostly green. But the lizards that wandered on to the rocky slope and made their home there would be more likely to evolve to be grey and speckled, to be better camouflaged among the rocks.

As each habitat naturally "selects" the lizards that suit it best, each ends up with its own type of lizard. Eventually, they will be so different that they are no longer one species, but two. This explains why species change from area to area.

It was Darwin who first used the phrase "natural selection" in his work on species. Wallace did not use it in the essay he wrote in Indonesia, although he described the same thing.

Natural selection is sometimes called "the survival of the fittest". Another scientist, Herbert Spencer, invented this phrase to describe Darwin's work. It can be confusing, because in modern English, "fit" mainly means strong and muscly. But "survival of the fittest" does not mean survival of the strongest. In fact, "survival of the fittest" means that the living things that survive are the *most suitable*. In other words, they suit or "fit" their habitat the best.

Darwin and Wallace both saw that farmers did something similar too. They chose, or selected, the most useful plants and animals for farming – such as the woolliest sheep, or the apple trees with the biggest fruit. They then used these for breeding, so as to keep the useful features and pass them on. Selective breeding turned wild sheep, wheat, apples and so on into different, more useful farm versions.

wild sheep ⟶ domesticated farm sheep

Darwin also wrote about another way things could evolve.
Besides being selected for features that help them survive, members of a species select each other as mates. Most species have young when a male and a female mate. So only those that can find a mate can reproduce and pass on their features.

This is important in species such as peacocks and birds of paradise. Males put on a colourful display to impress the females, and the females choose the best. Over time, these species evolve features like colourful tails or plumes or complex mating dances.

bird of paradise

Going public

Two scientists had worked out exactly how living things evolve. It was a huge step – but the idea had still not been made public. For scientists, in the 1850s as now, the most important thing was to publish your work. Published papers were a record of scientific ideas and of who had discovered what.

In June 1858, after a long journey, Wallace's letter and essay on evolution arrived at Darwin's house. Darwin was shocked by what had happened. He immediately sat down to write to Lyell.

Darwin thought that all his originality – his own ideas – would amount to nothing. But he tried to make the best of it. His book, full of evidence, examples and details, would still be interesting and important.

In his letter to Lyell, Darwin wrote, "Your words have come true with a vengeance. I never saw a more striking coincidence."

He enclosed Wallace's essay and begged Lyell to reply so that he could report back to Wallace. He also said he would help to get the paper published.

Lyell

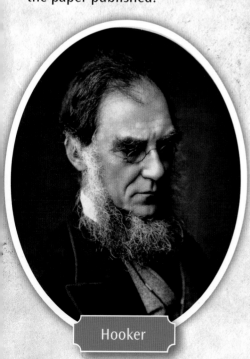

Hooker

As his son was ill with the deadly scarlet fever, Darwin left it to Lyell – and Darwin's best friend, the botanist Joseph Hooker – to decide what to do.

Darwin's delay

Darwin thought of natural selection around 1838, but didn't publish his idea for 20 years. This long wait is often called "Darwin's delay". Some people think Darwin didn't publish his idea because it was so scandalous, he was worried how people might react. Some even say he didn't want to upset his wife, Emma, or his old friend Robert FitzRoy, who were both very religious.

However, Darwin didn't actually keep his idea a secret. He shared the details with Emma and many of his friends. Plenty of important scientists, such as Charles Lyell and Joseph Hooker, knew all about it. In fact, these explanations are more likely:

- Darwin had lots of work to do. Through the 1840s and 1850s, he was writing books about his *Beagle* voyage. He also studied many other topics, such as barnacles and coral reefs.

- He wanted to write a detailed book on natural selection – not just an essay. That meant even more work to fit in.

- Having a wife and ten children took up a lot of his time.

- On top of all this, Darwin was unwell. Ever since his round-the-world trip, he'd suffered from a strange illness and couldn't always work. Today, experts think it was probably Chagas disease, which is spread by South America's biting bedbugs.

Despite his delay, Darwin knew his idea was important, so in 1844 he wrote a short outline to explain it. He gave instructions to Emma to have it published if he died unexpectedly.

When Lyell and Hooker saw Wallace's paper, they decided there was no time to waste – they must publish the theory of natural selection at once. They didn't even ask Wallace first. He was so far away that it would have taken months to write to him and receive a reply.

Instead, the two men took Darwin's outline of his theory from 1844, along with a letter he had written in 1857 to an American scientist, Asa Gray. Both of these explained his ideas on natural selection. They combined them with Wallace's essay to make a joint paper and sent it to the Linnean Society in London.

The Linnean Society still exists today. It is one of the world's most important societies for discussing and studying natural history. Lyell, Hooker and Darwin were all members of the club and it was due to hold a meeting on 1 July 1858.

The secretary agreed to present the new paper and it was read out at the meeting. Lyell and Hooker sat in the audience.

The stars of the show, though, were not there. Darwin's baby son had died on 28 June. Darwin was at home in Downe, unable to think of anything else. Wallace, meanwhile, was in the distant Asian jungle, completely unaware of what was happening.

Today, 1 July 1858 is remembered as a key moment in science history. It was the day when the theory of evolution by natural selection made its first official appearance. Eventually, it would become one of the biggest topics in science.

However, it did not have a huge impact straight away. This was partly because many of those who heard the paper read that night were scientists who already knew of Darwin's ideas.

19th-century news

In 1858 there was no internet, or even a phone network. News did not travel fast. No one could text about the amazing paper they had just heard, or put a copy online. It took time for people to hear about the idea and realise how important it was.

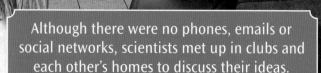

Although there were no phones, emails or social networks, scientists met up in clubs and each other's homes to discuss their ideas.

In August 1858, the Linnean Society published the Darwin-Wallace paper in print, as it did with all the essays read out at its meetings. In 1859, Linnean Society president Thomas Bell summed up the previous year. He obviously didn't think much of the Darwin-Wallace paper, as he remarked that there had not been any very interesting discoveries!

However, many other scientists found the new idea fascinating. Some changed their minds about evolution on the spot. The paper was soon printed in several other, more popular magazines too and word began to spread.

Great scientists

Both Wallace and Darwin thought of natural selection and the paper was published jointly in both their names. So why is Darwin's name now so much more likely to be linked to evolution?

One big reason is Darwin's book *The Origin of Species*. After the joint paper was published, Darwin's friends Lyell and Hooker urged him to finish a book on the subject once and for all. It was finally published in November 1859.

This was a much bigger event than the meeting the previous year. In fact, it made Darwin world-famous. News of natural selection had spread among scientists and they often discussed it. Now Darwin's book could give them all the details. It was very well written and easy to understand, and it became popular with the public too.

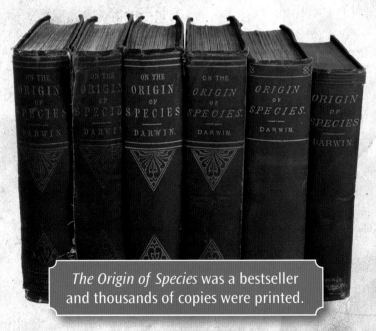

The Origin of Species was a bestseller and thousands of copies were printed.

Scientists, religious leaders and politicians all began debating the ideas in the book. It's often believed that it caused widespread outrage, but this isn't really true. A few people were outraged, but there were actually many different points of view.

They all had one thing in common, though – they focused on Darwin and his book, and not really on Wallace. Before long, the word "Darwinism" was being used to mean evolution. Darwin was the man of the moment.

Cartoons of Darwin appeared in the papers.

What Darwin and Wallace did next

Darwin was now 50 years old. As he was often unwell, it might have made sense to retire. Instead, he kept on working. He felt that *The Origin of Species* was really just a rough draft of his ideas, and he had much more to say.

He wrote about selective breeding and domestic animals, and how emotions and behaviour seemed similar in humans and animals. In his famous 1871 book *The Descent of Man*, he answered the question Wallace had asked him many years before, and described how humans must have evolved from apes.

Newspapers sometimes made jokes about Darwin, laughing at the idea that people were related to apes. However, Darwin was surprised to find that *The Descent of Man* was very popular. Evolution was no longer shocking – it was everyday science and most scientists accepted it. Darwin was reported as saying, "20 years ago such ideas would have ... been hooted at, but now ... everybody is talking about it without being shocked!"

At the same time, Darwin carried on with his other interests, making close studies of nature and writing up his discoveries. His later works included books on orchids, earthworms and meat-eating plants.

Wallace stayed in Southeast Asia for four more years. Joseph Hooker wrote to tell him that his paper had been published along with Darwin's work, and Wallace wrote back to say how grateful he was. But, he said, he could not be persuaded to leave his birds and insects and hurry home to England.

He finally returned in 1862, aged 39. One of the first things he did was to visit Darwin. The two became friends and often supported each other. Wallace went on to become just as famous as Darwin, as a scientist, thinker and writer.

Smile for the camera!

By the 1860s, the fairly new invention of photography had become widespread. As well-known scientists, Darwin and Wallace were photographed quite often. There are many photos of them in middle and old age, both with long beards.

Darwin in 1869

Wallace in 1895

Wallace did write books about natural selection, including one called *Darwinism*, published in 1869. He had many other interests too, like **hypnosis**, social issues such as poverty and **feminism**, the environment, and the possibility of life on other planets. In 1898, he wrote *The Wonderful Century*, a book about the great inventions, discoveries and ideas of the 1800s.

However, his most successful books were about his travels – especially *The Malay Archipelago*, published in 1869. This big, illustrated two-volume work described all the places Wallace visited on his eight-year Asian adventure. It told of beautiful landscapes, fabulous plants and animals, dangerous journeys and little-known peoples, and became a bestseller.

In 1908, when Wallace was 85, he was awarded a special medal for his life's work. It was the first ever Darwin-Wallace gold medal, set up by the Linnean Society to mark 50 years since the Darwin-Wallace paper was first presented. Today, the Darwin-Wallace medal is still awarded once a year for outstanding work on evolution.

Last years

Both Charles Darwin and Alfred Russel Wallace had long lives, especially Wallace, who lived to be 90. They both kept working and writing for as long as they could.

As he approached 70, Darwin wrote a private autobiography for his family to read. He was still studying and writing books, too. His last book, on worms, came out in 1871, when he was 72. Even after that he was still doing experiments on plants, with the help of his grown-up children.

By March 1882, Darwin was suffering serious pain and exhaustion. He had heart disease and grew weaker and weaker. He died on 19 April, aged 73.

The day before, Darwin had said to his wife Emma, "Remember what a good wife you have been." To his children he said, "There were never such good nurses as you."

Darwin thought he would be buried in his local cemetery in Downe. However, his scientific friends arranged for him to have a **state funeral** and to be buried in Westminster Abbey in London – an extremely rare honour. Newspapers, politicians and religious leaders all praised him, calling him "a glory to his country" and "the king of science".

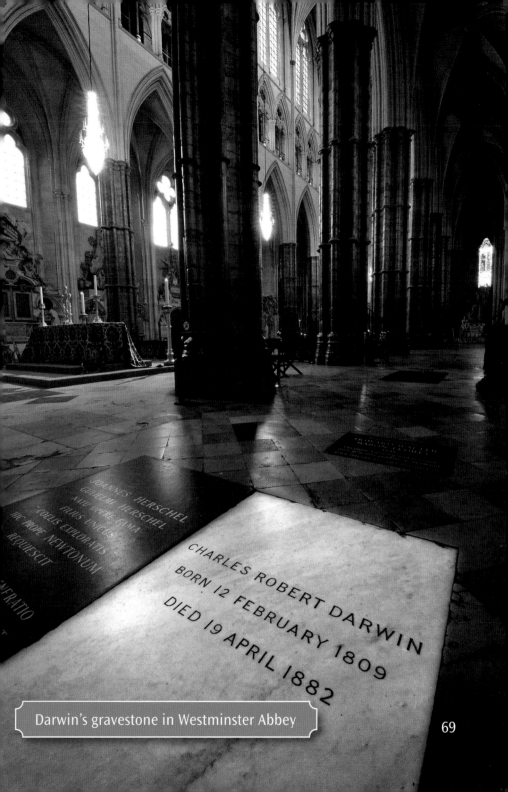

JOHANNES HERSCHEL
GUILELMI HERSCHEL
NATU OPERIB GIMA
FILIUS UNICUS
"COELIS EXPLORATIS"
HIC PROPE NEWTONUM
REQUIESCIT

CHARLES ROBERT DARWIN
BORN 12 FEBRUARY 1809
DIED 19 APRIL 1882

Darwin's gravestone in Westminster Abbey

Wallace lived for another 30 years after Darwin died. Besides writing and studying, he toured the USA and built several houses for his family. His last books were published in the year of his death, 1913, when he was 90.

In the summer of 1913, Wallace began to feel ill and weak. He died in his sleep early in the morning of 7 November, at home in Broadstone, on England's south coast.

By this time, Wallace was the best-known naturalist in Britain and one of the most famous scientists in the world. Some of his friends thought he should lie in Westminster Abbey alongside Darwin. However, he had asked to be buried quietly in Broadstone and his wife and children stuck to that plan.

Obituaries described Alfred Russel Wallace as "the greatest of all modern scientists" and "one of the giants of the wonderful century". Sadly, though, plans to make a statue of him had to be postponed, after the First World War broke out in 1914.

One hundred years after his death, the statue was finally built. It stands in the gardens of London's Natural History Museum and was unveiled in November 2013.

Inside the museum a statue of Darwin and a portrait of Wallace can be seen side by side.

Both men now have the recognition they deserve for their great gifts to science.

Leaving a legacy

The work of Charles Darwin and Alfred Russel Wallace has had a huge influence on modern science ever since. Thousands of great scientists have built on their ideas. One of the most important developments of all is the science of genetics, the study of genes and DNA – the chemical that genes are made of.

Though Darwin and Wallace discovered how evolution worked, they did not know how one living thing actually passes on its features to its children. How, for example, does a lizard actually pass on its own features, such as its green skin, to its young?

In the 1860s, while Darwin and Wallace were still alive, a monk named Gregor Mendel was studying this very problem. Working with pea plants and bees, he discovered important patterns in the way living things passed on their features, or traits. He realised that living things received instructions for each trait from their parents in the cells used to make seeds or young. Mendel called these instructions "factors".

Although Mendel's work was not well-known at the time, Darwin actually had a book in his library that mentioned Mendel's discoveries – but it's thought he never read it. However, around 1900, after Mendel's death, his ideas were rediscovered. With the help of new, better microscopes, scientists began looking inside cells to see how living things pass on their traits to their young – and found that Mendel was right.

Mendel at work in his monastery garden

Over the next 50 years, scientists found that cells contain long strings of a chemical called DNA. Sections of these strings, called genes, hold the instructions for traits like a lizard's green skin, a sheep's thick wool or a human's straight or curly hair. They are the "factors" Mendel described.

The information in DNA can change, thanks to mistakes that occur when cells copy themselves, and the complicated way genes are passed on. This explains the slight differences between living things that make evolution possible.

Today, evolution and genetics combined make up one of the biggest areas in science. Our knowledge of genes and how they evolve helps us understand many diseases, such as cancer. Scientists study how germs like the flu virus and hospital bugs evolve, so that we can fight them. We can even change living things by changing their genes, and identify people by their own unique DNA patterns.

a computer-generated image of a DNA molecule

Darwin and Wallace knew the discovery of natural selection was important. But what would they have made of where it has led us? They might have been surprised that Wallace became less well-known for a time, as he was so famous in his day. They would have been fascinated by the many debates and disagreements about evolution that are still going on.

Most of all, they would probably have been amazed to see all the different areas of science their ideas branched out into, just 150 years on from the announcement of their work. And they would have been thrilled to see how much more we have learnt – and are still learning – about living things.

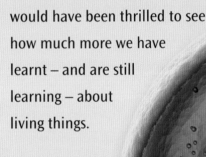

Today we know much more than Darwin and Wallace did about living things, such as what the insides of cells look like. For example, they had no idea that the inside of a cell looks like this.

Glossary

biologist   a scientist who studies living things

botany   the science of plants

clergymen   church leaders, like vicars and priests

feminism   the campaign for women to have equal rights with men

genes   the parts of cells that decide what characteristics a living thing will have

habitat   a place or set of conditions where something lives

hypnosis   a way of making people go into a sleep-like trance

inconsiderate   thoughtless or unkind

natural history   the science of living things

naturalists   people who study plants and creatures where these things live

obituaries   newspaper articles about someone's life, written shortly after they have died

philosopher   someone who studies ideas about truth and knowledge

pros and cons   points in favour and against

species   particular types of living thing

state funeral   a ceremonial funeral for a person of national importance

surveying   measuring and making maps of the Earth's surface

Index

Two men, one big idea

Charles Darwin

1809 Darwin is born.

1837
Darwin forms his ideas for how evolution works: "One species does change into another."

1856 Darwin and Wallace start writing to each other.

1831–1836 Darwin's trip to South America

1858 Wallace forms his ideas for how evolution works. The Darwin-Wallace paper is published.

1859 *The Origin of Species* is published.

1882 Darwin dies.

Alfred Russel Wallace

1823 Wallace is born.

1848–1852 Wallace's trip to South America

1853 Darwin and Wallace meet for the first time.

1854–1862 Wallace's trip to Southeast Asia

Today, their images are side by side in the Natural History Museum.

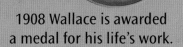

1908 Wallace is awarded a medal for his life's work.

1913 Wallace dies.

Ideas for reading

Written by Clare Dowdall, PhD
Lecturer and Primary Literacy Consultant

Learning objectives: check that the book makes sense, discuss understanding and explore the meaning of words in context; summarise the main ideas drawn from more than one paragraph, identify key details that support the main ideas; select appropriate grammar and vocabulary, understanding how such choices can change and enhance meaning

Curriculum links: Science

Interest words: natural selection, evolve, naturalists, endangered, specimens, transmutation, fanatical, warning colouration, habitat, legacy, genetics

Resources: ICT and whiteboards

Getting started

This book can be read over two or more reading sessions.

- Look at the front cover and read the title. Ask children if they have heard of Charles Darwin and Alfred Russel Wallace, and to share any ideas about them.

- Turn to the contents page. Ask children to read the contents in pairs to deduce what kind of men Darwin and Wallace were (great scientists), and in what field they worked (nature, evolution).

Reading and responding

- Explain that this book is a biography that will recount the lives of two famous scientists: Darwin and Wallace. Ask children to read pp 2–3 *Age of discovery* to find out when Darwin and Wallace lived, and what was special about them and these times. Help children to get a sense of the era by discussing what life might have been like then, and by connecting to children's existing understanding.